Edmund Edward Antrobus

The Prison And the School

Edmund Edward Antrobus

The Prison And the School

ISBN/EAN: 9783744761635

Printed in Europe, USA, Canada, Australia, Japan

Cover: Foto ©ninafisch / pixelio.de

More available books at **www.hansebooks.com**

THE PRISON AND THE SCHOOL.

SECOND NUMBER.

AN APPEAL FOR THE GIRLS.

BY

EDMUND EDWARD ANTROBUS, F.S.A.,

JUSTICE OF THE PEACE FOR THE COUNTY OF MIDDLESEX AND THE CITY AND
LIBERTY OF WESTMINSTER; CHAIRMAN OF THE STRAND DIVISION;
VISITING JUSTICE OF THE HOUSE OF CORRECTION, WESTMINSTER,
AND
THE MIDDLESEX INDUSTRIAL SCHOOL, FELTHAM.

LONDON:

STAUNTON & SON, 9, STRAND.

1871.

In the year 1853 the first number of the "Prison and the School" was printed for the consideration of the Magistrates of the County of Middlesex, and the kind reception it met with induces the writer of this the second number to hope that his colleagues will look over its pages not only for the sake of one who has been upwards of twenty years working with them, but more especially for the cause which is advocated in them.

INDEX.

THE PRISON AND THE SCHOOL.

Application to Parliament for Act to establish Industrial Schools, &c. In the year 1853 the Court of Quarter Session for the county of Middlesex, appointed a Special Committee to consider the expediency of making an application to Parliament for an Act to enable the Magistrates of the county to establish Industrial Schools for the reception and maintenance of juvenile offenders of the county; the Special Committee reported in favour of this step being taken, and the recommendation was adopted by the Court; in the following session, in the year 1854, an application was made, and the legislature passed the Middlesex Act, 17 and 18 Vic., c. clxix.

Appointment of a Special Committee to provide one or more Schools. After obtaining the Act the Court appointed a Special Committee to consider to what extent it would be advisable for the Magistrates to avail themselves of its provisions ; after due deliberation the Committee reported that it would be prudent to establish an Industrial School for boys only, at the time most urgently required ; the Court sanctioned the course proposed, and the Industrial School at Feltham was established, since which upwards of two thousand boys have been received within its walls ; more than seventy-five per cent. of those discharged have turned out well, proving the value of the Act, the success of its provisions, and the excellent management of the Institution.

Contract with Hampstead and Limpley Stoke Schools for the reception of girls.

The question of making some provision for girls was subsequently brought under the notice of the Court, and an arrangement was made with the managers of the Reformatory School at Hampstead, and also with one at Limpley Stoke, near Bristol.

Special Committee appointed by the Court, 1867.

In the year 1867, in consequence of the great difficulty of obtaining accommodation in the existing institutions, a Special Committee was appointed by the Court, and after due enquiry, the Committee reported to the Court on the county day of the May General Sessions, 1867,—

Report of Committee.

"That after minute enquiry, it appears to your Committee that an urgent necessity exists for making further provision for the class of female juvenile offenders in this county referred to in the order of the Court, the existing Reformatories being inadequate to the requirements of the county, and affording means for the reception and accommodation of only a very limited number of such female offenders as vacancies occur.

"Your Committee, in considering, as they were desired to do, what steps should be taken to provide for such cases, came to the opinion that it would be desirable that any such provision should be made under the Reformatory and Industrial Schools Acts, 1866 (29th and 30th Vict., caps. 117 and 118), and that the Court of Quarter Sessions, as the prison authority, should, under the 28th section of this Act, establish or build, or contribute towards the establishment or building, of a school, intended to be a certified Reformatory School on a limited scale, and capable of future extension, if necessary; some doubts, however, having been subequently suggested in respect to the powers given to Courts of Quarter Session, under the 28th section, your Committee directed that a case should be prepared and submitted to counsel, for his opinion as to whether the Court could establish and provide such a building, or were not precluded from doing more than contributing towards the establishment of a school, or towards the maintenance of an existing one. The case was laid before Mr. Hannen, and from his opinion, which, however, is not conclusive, your Committee were themselves quite satisfied that the Act gave the Court no authority to build or to originate or take the initiative in a Reformatory School, and the Committee at once entered into communication with the Secretary of State for the Home Department, trusting that if the powers were, as they believed, limited to the advancement of money, or to the support by weekly payments of money to existing institutions, he might be induced to increase the powers, so that the Courts of Quarter Session might originate them."

The following is a letter addressed to Mr. Secretary Hardy in reply to one of the 12th of June :—

Letter to the Home Secretary of State and reply.

" SIR,

" I am requested to acknowledge the receipt of your letter of the 12th instant, and in reply beg to state for the information of Mr. Secretary Hardy the especial object the Committee appointed by the Court of Quarter Sessions had in requesting an interview with him.

"In the year 1854 the Justices of the county of Middlesex obtained an Act of Parliament to enable them to erect and support Industrial Schools for the reception of juvenile offenders in the county of Middlesex; under this Act the Industrial School at Feltham was erected, and at present upwards of six hundred boys are inmates. In the year 1860 the Justices deemed it desirable to make some provision for girls, but as the Middlesex Act only provided for juvenile offenders under fourteen years of age, and as the far larger number of these cases are above that age the Justices availed themselves of the provisions of the general Act, 20 and 21 Vict., cap. 55, and entered into agreements with the managers of several certified Reformatories for the reception of county cases.

"At the present time, however, there are not any certified Reformatory Schools in the county available for the reception of girls, and the Justices think it may be advisable to make some permanent, instead of the present temporary, arrangement, and are therefore anxious to avail themselves of the provisions of the 29 and 30 Vict., cap. 117; in consequence, however, of there being some doubt as to the extent of the powers given them by the 28th section, an opinion of counsel has been taken, which appears to confirm the received interpretation that their powers are confined to contributing only towards Reformatory Schools already provided or to be provided by others.

"After mature consideration of the subject, the Committee, of which I am the chairman, are of opinion that the object the legislature has in view would be materially advanced, and the proceedings under the Reformatory Schools Act of last session simplified, if power were given to the Justices to institute and maintain, with the sanction and under the control of the Home Office, such schools, instead of merely contributing to existing institutions. Should Mr. Secretary Hardy, after deliberation, coincide with the Committee in the view they have taken, the object, it appears to them, could be accomplished by passing a short Act, amending and explanatory of the 29 and 30 Vict., cap. 117, during the present session.

"I am, Sir,
"Your obedient Servant,
(Signed) "EDMD. E. ANTROBUS.
"E. A. Perceval, Esq."

To which the following reply was received:—

"Whitehall, July 1, 1867.
"SIR,
"I am directed by Mr. Secretary Hardy to acknowledge the receipt of your letter of the 17th ultimo, representing that the Committee appointed by the Court of Quarter Sessions for Middlesex are anxious to take the necessary steps for providing a Reformatory School for girls in the county, but are hindered by the belief that the provisions of the 29 and 30 Vict., cap. 117, limit their powers to contributing only towards a Reformatory School already provided or to be provided by others.

"It appears to Mr. Hardy that the Committee have been correctly informed as to the interpretration of the Act, and that the continued use of the word 'contribute,' shows clearly that the prison authority is not intended to take the initiative, and throw the whole expense upon the county; there must be an existing undertaking which requires their assistance. Mr. Hardy does not consider that there is any call for further legislation upon the subject at present, nor, indeed, if there were, would there be time for it in the course of the present session.

" I am, Sir,

" Your obedient Servant,

" H. WADDINGTON.

" Edmund E. Antrobus, Esq., J.P.,

   " Sessions House, Clerkenwell."

"Under these circumstances, your Committee endeavoured to ascertain if there was any prospect of establishing Industrial Schools or Reformatories, under the General Acts, 29 and 30 Vict., caps. 117 and 118, as now constituted, by means of private funds, but after due enquiry and consideration, your Committee are satisfied there is no prospect of this being accomplished.

Report of Special Committee, Nov. 25, 1869.

" Your Committee beg to remind the Court that it was the intention of the Magistrates, when the application was made to the legislature for the Middlesex Industrial School Act, to erect schools for both boys and girls, and that the legislature contemplated provision being made for juvenile offenders of both sexes, but that after the Act was obtained, the Committee appointed to carry out its provisions, considered it advisable to postpone for a time the establishment of a girls' school, and in which resolution the Court concurred.

"Your Committee, under these circumstances, are of opinion that the time has arrived for provision being made for girls, and that an Industrial School should be provided under the Middlesex Act, other means proving impracticable, in some convenient locality, for a limited number of female juvenile offenders, in as economical a manner as a due regard to efficiency will permit, with a view to obtain a Government certificate hereafter, for the whole or a portion of the proposed school under the Reformatory or Industrial Schools Act, 29 and 30 Vict., caps. 117 and 118.

"EDMUND E. ANTROBUS,

"Chairman.

"Sessions House, 25 November, 1867."

This report was presented to the Court on the 28th of November, 1867, and was printed and circulated in the usual way, and taken into consideration on the county day in January, 1868.

Third Report of Special Committee, March 30, 1868.

A third report was presented to the Court on the county day in the following April.

"In compliance with the instructions given to your Committee by the Court in January last, they have further considered the probable extent of the requirements of the county as to the establishment of a Girls' Reformatory, and they now append an extract from the tenth report of the Inspector of Reformatories, from which it appears that the experience of all the Reformatories, both in England and Scotland, both Protestant and Roman Catholic, proves that the accommodation required for girls is about one-fourth of that wanted for boys; and that inasmuch as the Boys' School at Feltham, with a provision for 800, has never yet been filled, it would appear to be fair to conclude that a provision for 200 girls would be ample for the requirements of the county; and of this number about 100 are at present accommodated in the Hampstead and Limpley Stoke schools, leaving little more than 100 to be provided for. In what manner such provision should be made is a question probably beyond the province of this Committee; but unless suitable premises can be secured at a moderate rent, they venture to suggest that the system recently adopted at the 'Little Boys' Home,' near Farningham, would be worthy of careful consideration.

"This system is that of the erection of several small houses capable of containing 30 inmates each, with a central building to be used as a school-chapel. The whole to be placed in, say four to six acres of land, so as to allow a drying ground to be attached to each house.

"There appears to exist much misapprehension in the minds of some Magistrates as to the advantages obtained under the public Act, by other places. The county has obtained for the boys sent to Feltham, under the Industrial Schools Act, of 1866, all the advantages, including the Treasury grant, which are obtained by any other school whatsoever; and in the event of a Girls' School being established by the county under the Middlesex Act, and certified under the Reformatory Schools Act, of 1866, the same result would necessarily follow for all girls committed to such schools under the last Act quoted.

"The major part of the amendments which were

sought for the Middlesex Act, 1865, including the Treasury grant, have since been obtained for one-half of the Feltham School, by the certificate under the Industrial Schools Act, of 1866, and the limitation of these benefits to one half of the school was the act of the Court itself, by a resolution of the 22nd November, 1866.

"An Amendment of the Public Industrial and Reformatory Act, of 1866, inviting counties to initiate schools under those Acts, instead of merely empowering them to supplement the funds when they are established by voluntary effort, would greatly simplify and facilitate the establishment of the class of schools sought for; but inasmuch as the Government have hitherto declined so to amend the public Acts, and inasmuch as no Reformatory School for girls exists in the neighbourhood of London which could be adopted and supplemented by the county, other than the Hampstead School, the managers of which do not wish to extend their operations, your Committee see only one alternative to the recommendation in their former report, that a Reformatory School for girls should be established under the Middlesex Act, with the view of obtaining a certificate under the Reformatory Act, 1866 — namely, that such schools should be, in the first instance, started by a few independent promoters, who may be willing to incur some amount of trouble and a limited expenditure, leaving it to the Court to aid the scheme by whatever additional outlay was requisite, as by the Reformatory School Act, of 1866, they would be enabled to do.

"If, therefore, a few Magistrates, or other persons interested in the matter, would subscribe to originate a Female Reformatory School for Middlesex, it will be within the province of the Court of Quarter Sessions, as the 'Prison Authority' under the Act, to contribute such sums of money towards the establishment or building of the school, and subsequently towards the support of the inmates of the school as in its wisdom it may think fit.

"This course has recently been pursued by the Magistrates of the county of Stafford, and by the Town Council of Birmingham, for schools for which Government certificates have already been granted.

"As to the conditions on which the Court would contribute any such sums of money, it would probably be considered necessary that the property purchased should be vested in the county.

"Your Committee trust that when the facilities which the Act affords are fully known there will not be wanting subscribers to take the initiative in bringing the enactments into operation.

"Should such an effort be made, the suggested recourse to the Middlesex Act would be rendered unnecessary.

"EDMUND E. ANTROBUS,
"Chairman.

"March 30, 1868."

This latter report was taken into consideration on the county day in May, when the following resolution was passed :—

Re-appointment of the Special Committee. "That the Committee be re-appointed, and that the subject be referred back to the Committee with instructions to see whether a school for female juvenile offenders can be

erected under the general Act, and for that purpose
to invite subscriptions to initiate the undertaking."

In order to comply with the resolution of the
Court, the following letter was addressed to the
Magistrates of the county by the Special Com-
mittee:—

Letter to the
Magistrates of
the county of
Middlesex.
" Sessions House, Clerkenwell,
" June 22nd, 1868.
" SIR,

" On the county day of the General
Sessions in May, 1867, the Court appointed a Special
Committee to consider the want of accommodation in
certified Reformatory Schools for female juvenile
offenders in Middlesex, and as the two reports, dated
the 25th November, 1867, and 30th March, 1868, presented to the Court, have been printed and circulated
among the Magistrates of the county, they are already
aware that an urgent necessity exists for making
further provision for this class of offenders, particularly
for those between the ages of fourteen and sixteen
years.

" At the last county day the Court re-appointed
the Committee, with instructions to see whether a
school for female juvenile offenders can be established
under the General Act, and for that purpose to invite
subscriptions to initiate the undertaking.

" Under the Middlesex Industrial School Act, the
Court have the power to purchase land, and establish
and support industrial schools for juvenile offenders
under the age of fourteen years. A school, however,
under this Act would, with respect to girls, be very
limited in its operation, as it would exclude girls

B

between the ages of fourteen and sixteen years, for whom provision is especially required, and the entire cost of the maintenance would, moreover, be thrown on the county.

"It has accordingly been suggested by the Court in their last resolution, that without adopting this Act, with its limited operation, and its large liabilities, that efforts should be made to establish a Reformatory School under the Reformatory Schools Act, 1866, which gives the power desired, of receiving girls up to the age of sixteen years, and entitles the school to the Treasury allowance towards its support and maintenance. To carry the above suggestion into effect, it is, however, requisite that some sum of money should be, in the first instance, raised, as a basis for initiating the undertaking by a subscription among the Magistrates, such sum to be supplemented, if the Court think proper, by a grant out of the County Rate, without which assistance the measure will not be prosecuted, and contributors, therefore, will be in no event answerable for any amount whatever beyond the sums subscribed.

"Under these circumstances, the Committee submit the scheme to your favourable consideration, and will be glad to learn whether you are disposed to support the undertaking, and if so, to what amount.

"I am, Sir,
"Your obedient Servant,
"Edmund E. Antrobus,
"Chairman."

Result of the appeal contained in the letter.   This appeal to the Magistrates was not successful. Notwithstanding the efforts made by the Committee to obtain sub-

scriptions, only £290 were offered as contributions.
The Committee did not despair of being able to obtain
funds ultimately, sufficient to meet the requirements
of the Act, and presented the following Report to the
Court:—

First indepen-   In order to meet the requirement of
dent Committee. the General Acts, an Independent Committee was formed, but this Committee
did not take any steps to obtain funds for the establishment of a school.

Report presented to the Court, February General
Sessions, 1869:—

" The Committee, acting under the instructions of
the Court, have, since their last Report, endeavoured
to obtain funds for the establishment of a Reformatory
School for girls, to be certified under the 29th and
30th Vict., cap. 117, and towards which the sum of
£300 has been promised by the Magistrates of the
county. Before reporting the result of their appeal,
the Committee caused an advertisement to be inserted
in the public papers for premises, which might be
eligible for an institution of this character, and ac-
ceptable to the Court, but the application was not,
however, successful, in consequence, in a great degree,
of houses and premises of the extent required, in
eligible localities, being, at the expiration of existing
leases, pulled down, and the sites let for building
villas or streets, the ground attached to them being
ot more value for this purpose than the old and usually
inconvenient houses upon it.

" Your Committee, appreciating the difficulty of

establishing a school under the Reformatory Act of 1866, again addressed a letter to the Home Secretary of State, requesting his attention to the provisions of the Act, and their reconsideration, but they regret to add that the request contained in their letter has not been complied with. The following are copies of the letter and reply:—

Second letter to the Home Secretary of State, Jan. 27, 1869, and reply.

" ' Sessions House, Clerkenwell,

" ' 27 January, 1869.

" ' SIR,

" ' On the 11th of June, 1867, I had the honour, as chairman of a Special Committee of Justices appointed by the Court of Quarter Sessions for the county of Middlesex, to address a letter to Mr. Secretary Hardy respecting the difficulty which existed in finding certified Reformatory School accommodation for girls convicted at the Sessions, Police Courts, and Petty Sessions of the county. The Justices were then anxious to avail themselves of the provisions of the 29th and 30th Vict., cap. 117, but were prevented doing so by the limited nature of the powers given under that Act; and they therefore suggested that the Court of Quarter Sessions should have power given them to originate Reformatory Schools, instead of merely contributing towards their erection and support. Mr. Secretary Hardy, however, in consequence of the recent amendment of the law as regards Reformatory Schools by that Act, did not consider it advisable to introduce any measure for a further alteration under the then existing circumstances.

" ' The great want of accommodation continuing, the Justices have, during the last year, been endeavouring to obtain funds by voluntary contributions for the formation of a Reformatory School, to be certified under the present Act; but, notwithstanding every effort, have been unable to obtain sufficient to accomplish this object. This, combined with the responsibilities it would entail, induces them to believe that there is not any prospect of establishing an institution for the county of Middlesex under the provisions of the Act with its present limitations.

"'Under these circumstances, and the urgent necessity of meeting the pressing evil, the Justices trust that the provisions of the Act may be reconsidered and so far amended as to empower the Court of Quarter Sessions to originate the establishment of Reformatory Schools in Middlesex.

"'I have also to request that you will be pleased to receive a deputation of members of the Committee on the subject, and appoint a time when they will be favoured with an interview.

"' I have the honour to remain,
"' Sir,
"' Your obedient Servant,
"' EDMUND E. ANTROBUS,
"' Chairman.
"' The Right Hon. H. A. Bruce, M.P.,
"' Secretary of State for the Home Department."

"' Whitehall,
"' February 2, 1869.
"' SIR,
"' I am directed by Mr. Secretary Bruce to acknowledge the receipt of your letter of the 27th ult., respecting the want of reformatory accommodation, for girls in the county of Middlesex; and I am to

acquaint you that, in the present state of public
business, Mr. Bruce is unable to receive a deputation
as you request, and that he concurs in the view taken
by Mr. Hardy of this subject in a letter addressed to
you on the 5th of March last.

     " ' I am, Sir,

      " ' Your obedient Servant,

       " ' A. F. O. LIDDELL.

" ' Edmund E. Antrobus, Esq., J.P.

   " ' 14, Kensington Palace Gardens.'

"Your Committee have further to report that, on
endeavouring to proceed under the Reformatory
Schools Act, 1866, they have found it impossible to
enter into satisfactory negotiations either for the
purchase or renting of existing premises, not having
any authority to do so. This impediment would be
removed if the Court would contribute, under the
powers given them by the Act of the 29th and 30th
Vict., cap. 117, s. 28, a sum of money towards the
establishment of a building for a certified Reformatory School, which would entitle the county to
the Government grant towards the support of the
inmates.

"Unless the Court comply with this suggestion,
the Committee see no other course than to proceed
under the Middlesex Act, according to the recommendation contained in their Report to the Court on
the county day of May, 1867, namely, that provision
should be made under the Middlesex Act, other means
proving impracticable, in some convenient locality,
for a limited number of female juvenile offenders, in
as economical a manner as a due regard to efficiency
will permit, with a view to obtain a Government

certificate under the provisions of the Reformatory or Industrial Schools Acts, 29th and 30th Vict., cap. 117 and 118.

"EDMUND E. ANTROBUS,

"Chairman."

Report of the Clerk of the Peace.
On the county day, 15th of July, 1869, "The Clerk of the Peace reported that he had caused advertisements to be published in the following public newspapers— viz., 'The Morning Herald,' of the 14th May last, and the 'Times,' of the 15th May last, of the intention of the Court on this day to take into consideration the making of a contribution, under 28th section of the Reformatory Schools Act, 1866, of a sum not exceeding £6,000 towards the establishment of a Reformatory School for female juvenile offenders, or to lease premises at an annual rent not exceeding £300 per annum.

Resolution to contribute 6,000l., or 300l. per annum towards the establishment of a Reformatory School.
"Edmund E. Antrobus, Esq., moved, pursuant to notice, 'That the Special Committee, appointed by the Court to consider the want of accommodation in certified Reformatory Schools for juvenile offenders in Middlesex, be authorized to contribute a sum not exceeding £6,000 for the purchase of a house and premises for a Reformatory School for girls, under the 29 and 30 Vict., cap. 117, or to lease premises at an annual rent not exceeding £300 per annum,' which was duly seconded, whereupon Thomas Turner, Esq., moved, by way of amendment, 'That this Court will contribute a sum not exceeding £6,000 towards the purchase of a house

and premises for a Reformatory School for girls, under the 29 and 30 Vict., cap. 117, on a proper scheme for the purpose being submitted by the Special Committee to and approved by the Court,' which amendment was duly seconded, and, on a division, carried. The same amendment was then put as a substantive motion, whereupon H. M. Kemshead, Esq., moved, by way of amendment, 'That the consideration of the question be adjourned to the county day of next October Quarter Session,' which was duly seconded, and put to the vote, but on a division lost; the first amendment was then put as an original motion, and carried.

" On the motion of Edmund E. Antrobus, Esq., which was duly seconded, the Special Committee appointed by the Court to consider the want of accommodation in certified Reformatory Schools for juvenile offenders in Middlesex, was re-appointed.

Report of Special   " On the county day, April 1870, the
Committee.   report from the Special Committee appointed by the Court to consider the want of accommodation in certified Reformatory Schools for female juvenile offenders at Middlesex, laid before the Court on the last county day was considered. The Clerk of the Peace reported, 'That in compliance with the provisions of the Act 29 and 30 Vict., cap. 117, he had given due notice, by advertisement, of the intention of the Court to take into consideration the making of a contribution under the 28th section of the Reformatory Schools Act, 1866, of a sum not exceeding £6,000 towards the establish-

ment of a Reformatory School for female juvenile offenders.'

Resolution to contribute 6,000*l.* for the purchase of Fortescue House.

"Capt. O'Brien having moved, pursuant to notice, and the same having been duly seconded, it was resolved,—'That a sum of £6,000 be contributed by the Middlesex Quarter Sessions towards the establishment of a Reformatory School for girls, by the purchase of Fortescue House, Twickenham, together with about an acre of land, the fitting and furnishing of the house for the accommodation of 100 girls, and the wages of the necessary staff, and the expenses of maintenance until the institution can be got into working order.'

"On the motion of Capt. O'Brien, which was duly seconded, it was resolved,—'That the county Treasurer be directed to pay the said sum of £6,000 to Trustees, to be appointed by the Court, in trust for the purposes of the school, and subject thereto in trust for the county of Middlesex.'

"On the motion of Capt. O'Brien, which was duly seconded, it was resolved 'That such Trustees be—

" 'The Chairman of the Court,
" 'Chairman of the Committee of Accounts,
" 'P. Northall Laurie, Esq.'

"On the motion of Captain O'Brien, which was duly seconded, it was resolved,—'That a Committee be formed for the purpose of carrying into effect the above resolution of the Court, for the establishment of a Reformatory School for girls.'"

The power to appoint trustees, or a Committee to manage a Reformatory School established under the 29 and 30 Vict., cap. 117, does not exist, and the course adopted was under an erroneous impression of the provisions.

The Report of the Special Committee appointed on the 28th of April last, &c. :—-

"On the county day of the Easter Quarter Session (the 28th of April), the Court resolved—'That the sum of £6000 be contributed by the Middlesex Quarter Session towards the establishment of a Reformatory School for girls, by the purchase of Fortescue House, Twickenham, together with about an acre of land, the fitting and furnishing of the house for the accommodation of 100 girls, the wages of the necessary staff, and the expense of maintenance until the institution can be got into working order;' and an order was made on the County Treasurer to pay the said sum of £6,000 to trustees, to be appointed by the Court, in trust for the purposes of the school, and, subject thereto, in trust for the county of Middlesex.

"Some doubt, however, being entertained by the County Treasurer as to whether the Quarter Sessions had power to make the order so made upon him, and whether he could safely pay the £6,000 in the manner and for the purposes specified therein, he prepared and submitted a case to Mr. Mellish, Q.C., and Mr. Channell, Q.C., upon the point, and their joint opinion thereon he laid before the Court on the 26th of May last, when such case and opinion were referred to your Committee to consider, and to report thereon to the Court.

"It will be in the recollection of the Court that a

case had been previously submitted on the subject to Mr. Hannen (now Mr. Justice Hannen), who was of opinion that the Court, as the prison authority, have power to purchase land for, and to establish and wholly maintain such a school. The joint opinion, however, now given by Mr. Mellish and Mr. Channell, being at variance with that given by Mr. Justice Hannen, your Committee recommend, in consequence of these conflicting opinions, that the course suggested by Mr. Mellish and Mr. Channell should be followed, of applying to the Court of Queen's Bench for a mandamus against the County Treasurer to show cause why he refused to obey the order of the Court so made upon him, for the purpose of obtaining an authoritative decision on the question raised by the County Treasurer, with respect to the validity of such order.

" ' Sessions House, Clerkenwell,

" ' 6 July, 1870.'

" Moved that the Report be received.

" ' That in consequence of the conflicting opinions which have been laid before the Court, the course suggested by Mr. Mellish and Mr. Channell be adopted and followed, of applying to the Court of Queen's Bench for a mandamus against the County Treasurer to show cause why he refuses to obey the order of the Court of the 28th of April last, for the payment of the sum of £6,000, towards the establishment of a Reformatory School for girls, for the purpose of obtaining an authoritative decision on the question raised by the County Treasurer with respect to the validity of such order ; and that the requisite steps be taken by the Clerk of the Peace for carrying the foregoing resolution into effect.' "

Sixth Report
of the Special
Committee,
Aug. 1870.

"At the last county day (the 14th July last) the Court directed the Clerk of the Peace to take the necessary steps, and to apply to the Court of Queen's Bench for a mandamus against the County Treasurer to show cause why he refused to obey the order of the Court of April 28th to pay the sum of £6,000 to trustees towards the establishment of a Reformatory School for girls by the purchase of Fortescue House, Twickenham, together with about an acre of land, the fitting and furnishing of the house for the accommodation of 100 girls, and the wages of the necessary staff, and the expense of maintenance until the institution could be got into working order. Since these directions were so given by the Court, a letter has been received from Dr. Rumsey to the effect that he has disposed of Fortescue House and the portion of land that he was offering to your Committee, and inasmuch as all the proceedings of your Committee since its formation, and the orders of Court connected therewith, have been based on the presumption that Fortescue House would be purchased from Dr. Rumsey, your Committee have no alternative but to recommend to the Court that the scheme be abandoned, and that the resolution of the Court of 28th April last, granting conditionally the sum of £6,000 towards the establishment of a Reformatory School for girls, and also the resolution of the Court of the 14th of July last, by which the Clerk of the Peace was instructed to apply for a mandamus against the County Treasurer, be rescinded. Your Committee, in coming to these conclusions, regret much that these endeavours to establish so useful an institution as the Fortescue House Reformatory for girls convicted of offences in

Middlesex, should have failed, through adverse circumstances which they could not have foreseen, especially after it had received the sanction of the Secretary of State. The want still remains; the condition of the young females convicted of offences is very deplorable, and demands early amelioration; and as in the present state of the law it is at least doubtful whether or not, under the General Act, the magisterial body can practically originate, as well as carry on, an adequate establishment for this purpose; your Committee hope and believe individuals may be found willing and ready to join in so excellent a work.

"D. O'Brien,
"Chairman.

" Sessions House, Clerkenwell,
"15th August, 1870."

" On the county day, October, 1870, the Report of the Special Committee appointed on the 28th of April last, to establish a Reformatory School for girls, laid before the Court on the last county day was considered.

Collapse of the scheme for the purchase of Fortescue House.

" Captain O'Brien moved, pursuant to notice, and the same having been duly seconded, it was resolved, 'That the scheme for the establishment of a Reformatory School for girls by the purchase of Fortescue House, be abandoned; the resolution of the Court of Quarter Session of the 28th of April, for contributing the sum of £600, be rescinded.'

" Captain O'Brien also moved, pursuant to notice, and the same having been duly seconded, it was resolved, ' That the resolution of the Court of the 14th of July last, by which the Clerk of the Peace was instructed to apply to the Court of Queen's Bench for a mandamus against the County Treasurer, to show cause why he refused to obey the order of Court for the payment of the sum contributed, of £6000, be rescinded.'

Second independent Committee. " In order fully to give effect to the recommendation of the Court, that efforts should be made to establish a school for female juvenile offenders in the county, and to invite subscriptions for this purpose to initiate the undertaking, a second independent Committee, required by the General Acts, was formed, notwithstanding the ill success which attended the former, and in reply to the following letter addressed to the Magistrates from the Committee, viz. :—

Edmund Edward Antrobus, Esq., J.P., Chairman.
The Rt. Hon. The Marquis of Westminster.
Henry Pownall, Esq., Chairman of the Quarter Sessions.
Sir William Henry Bodkin, Assistant Judge.
John Gilliam Stilwell, Esq., J.P.
John Norbury, Esq., J.P.
John Gilbert Talbot, Esq., M.P., J.P.
Thomas Lucas, Esq., J.P.
George Moore, Esq., J.P.
John T. France, Esq., J.P.
Henry John Baxter, Esq., J.P.
Benjamin John Armstrong, Esq., J.P.
James Holbert Wilson, Esq., J.P.
Henry Griffith, Esq., J.P.
Henry Edw. Pellew, Esq., J.P.

Robert Dimsdale, Esq., M.P., J.P.
Sir James Tyler, J.P.
General Tremenheere, J.P.
H. H. Seymour, Esq., J.P.
J. E. L. Brandreth, Esq., J.P.

" ' Sessions House, Broad Sanctuary,
" ' Westminster, 11th June, 1870.
" ' DEAR SIR,

" ' On the county day of the General Sessions, in May, 1867, the Court appointed a Special Committee to consider the want of accommodation in certified Reformatory Schools for female juvenile offenders in the county of Middlesex, and as the two Reports, dated the 25th of November, 1867, and the 30th March, 1868, presented to the Court, have been printed and circulated among the Magistrates of the county. They are already aware that an urgent necessity exists for making further provision for this class of offenders, a necessity fully recognized by the Court of Quarter Sessions. At the present time it has been ascertained that the need is even more urgent for the establishment of schools for the reception of girls, to be certified under the 29th and 30th Vict., caps. 117 and 118, the former more particularly for girls between the ages of fourteen and sixteen, and the latter for girls under fourteen years. A school certified under cap. 118 will provide for a class of girls identical, as regards age, with that of the boys who are now sent to the county Industrial School at Feltham, and being established under the provisions of the 29th and 30th Vict., cap. 118, it will be an institution in some important respects similar to the Feltham School, and to which Magistrates will have power to send young offenders, without their having to undergo a previous imprisonment. The Court of Quarter Sessions not having the power to originate Reformatory or Industrial Schools under the Statutes before named, the Committee proposes that efforts should be made to obtain by subscription a sufficient sum to purchase a site, and erect two buildings of a domestic character, each capable of receiving fifty inmates, and the requisite staff of officers, and thus to secure the means of adequate classification. In the first instance, however, it is proposed to establish and obtain a certificate for only one school, most probably a Reformatory School. This effected, the Court of Quarter Session will have the power to contribute, under the provisions of the Statute, such sums of money, and on such conditions as they think fit towards the alteration, enlargement, or re-building of a certified Reformatory or Industrial School, or towards the support of the inmates of such a school, or towards the management of such a school, or towards the establishment or building of a school intended to be a certified Reformatory or Industrial School, or towards the purchase of land, required either for the use of an existing Reformatory or Industrial School, or for the site of a school intended to be certified. A school or schools, when certified, will not only be in a position to receive support from the Court of Quarter Sessions, but to obtain the Government grant. It is intended that the schools should be Church of England Schools, under the control of a Committee of Managers, and that especial care should be taken to train the girls in industrial occupations, and to fit them for household work, either as servants in families, or in their own houses, when they leave the Institution.

" ' More has been done by the county of Middlesex for boys who have come under the law than by any other county, and with the most satisfactory results, but very little indeed for girls, the Committee therefore appeal to their brother Magistrates to lend their aid to rescue girls charged—many with slight offences, some almost children—from the disgrace of a prison ; girls who, in a vast number of cases, have been the victim of neglect, or the evil influence of persons with whom unfortunately they have been associated, and who, by timely care, may be rescued from a life of infamy and degradation, to become useful and respectable members of society.

" ' The Committee trust that a kind response will be made to their appeal by the Magistrates of the county, and that a sufficient sum of money will be contributed to enable the Committee to carry out this urgent and necessary work.

   " ' I have the honor to remain,
    " ' Dear Sir,
     " ' Yours faithfully,
      " ' EDMUND E. ANTROBUS,
       " ' Chairman.' "

Result of letter from independent Committee. To which a liberal response was made, and a sum of nearly eight hundred pounds contributed. It was, however, felt by a large number of Magistrates that any efforts made to supply the required wants by private means must prove inadequate in the Metropolitan county, and further, that any Institution established under either the general Acts, 29 and 30 Vict., caps. 117 or

118, must leave a large number of cases which would not properly or beneficially come under the operation of either unprovided for, but which would come under the excellent provisions of the Middlesex Act.

Notice of motion for a Special Committee to provide a school under the Middlesex Act. The following notice of motion was therefore given on the county day, November, 1870, and on the 12th of January, 1871:—A Committee was appointed to provide an Industrial School for the reception of girls, being juvenile offenders in the county of Middlesex, under the provisions of the 17th and 18th Vict., cap. 169.

Appointment of Committee. This Committee was unanimously appointed.

In April last the Committee made the following report :—

Report of Special Committee. " The Court having, under the authority of the 4th section of the statute, determined on providing a separate county Industrial School for females, and appointing a separate Committee for the purpose of erecting, providing, and managing such county female Industrial School, your Committee held their first meeting on the 3rd of February last, which was duly convened in the manner prescribed by the Act, and as required by the 6th section, they then elected a Chairman and appointed a Clerk.

" The first step which became necessary on the part of your Committee was, of course, that of obtaining a suitable site for the proposed School, and although more than one was offered to them which appeared in every way well adapted for the purpose,

still your Committee were of opinion that it would
be more satisfactory to the Court, that efforts should
be made to secure a site by public tender, and they
therefore caused the following advertisement to be
published in several of the daily newspapers : —

" Land to purchase—
" Wanted from 20 to 25 acres of land within a
radius of 20 miles from Charing Cross, or about
5 acres within the Metropolis, as defined by the
Metropolis Local Management Acts, the powers of
the Lands Clauses Consolidation Act, of 1845, relating
to the purchase of land by agreement being applicable,
may offer advantages to some trustees who are not
otherwise empowered to sell. Proposals stating the
locality, tenure, nature of the soil, means of drainage,
supply of water, and distance from the nearest railway station, are to be sent sealed up and addressed
to the Chairman of the Special Committee of Justices,
under cover to the Sessions House, Clerkenwell, on
or before Saturday the 25th instant.'

Land at Feltham
recommended
to the Court for
the site of the
proposed school.

" In pursuance of that advertisement,
thirty tenders of land were received, most
of which, however, from various causes,
were deemed altogether ineligible, or
could not be entertained on account of
the price required being excessive. The site which
appears to your Committee to be in many important
and essential points the most suitable among those
offered, is one at Feltham, a few hundred yards from
the Feltham station of the South Western Railway,
adjoining Hanworth Park estate; it consists of 17
acres of freehold land, the price asked being, in the

first instance, £280 per acre; but after some negoti-
ation between the Chairman of your Committee and
Mr. Francis Kent Junr., of Castle House, Hampton,
by whom the offer was made, he ultimately expressed
his willingness to accept £250 pound per acre; upon
which terms your Committee have agreed to purchase
the land in question, subject to the same being sanction by the Court, and approved by the Secretary of
State for the Home Department; and your Committee therefore have to request the Court to sanction
such purchase, subject to the approval of the Home
Secretary of State being obtained.

" EDMUND E. ANTROBUS,
" Chairman.

" This Report was taken into consideration on the
county day in May last, and the following amendment
to the proposed resolution was passed :—

Amendment to the resolution. " Upon the following resolution being
moved—'That the Committee appointed
by the Court, on the 12th of January last,
to provide an Industrial School for female juvenile
offenders of the county of Middlesex, under the provisions of the 17th and 18th Vict. cap. 169, be authorised
to enter into a contract, subject to the approval of the
Home Department, for the purchase of 17 acres of
land at Feltham, in this county, for the purpose of
erecting thereon such Industrial School at a sum not
exceeding £4,250'; the same was duly seconded, and
thereupon Captain Francis Morley moved by way of
amendment, which was carried,—' That, as the proposed school will, by the Middlesex Industrial School
Act, be entirely limited to convicted female juvenile

offenders, between 7 and 14 years of age only ; and, as no returns or information of their number has been laid before the Court, the consideration of this subject be postponed, until such information be produced as to show the necessity of incurring this large expenditure, and also the effect of the operations of the new School Board be ascertained.' "

"In compliance with the directions of the Court, the following letter was addressed to the Chairman of the Elementary Education Board:—

" ' Sessions House, Clerkenwell,

Letter to the
Elementary
School Board.

" ' June, 1871.

" ' My Lord,

" ' At the Quarter Sessions, in January last, the Court of Quarter Sessions appointed a Special Committee to establish an Industrial School for the reception of girls, under the provisions of the 17 and 18 Vict., cap. 169. Before, however, proceeding with the work, the Court has directed the Committee to ascertain if the Elementary Education 'Board intend to establish schools for the reception of girls under the provisions of 33 and 34 Vict., cap. 75, sec. 21.

" ' As the future proceedings of the Magistrates will be much influenced by the course taken by the Elementary School Board, I shall feel much obliged by being informed whether the Board contemplate taking any action under that section of the Act.

" ' I have the honour to remain,

" ' Your Lordship's most obedient Servant,

" ' EDMUND E. ANTROBUS, J.P.,

" ' Chairman of the Committee.

" ' The Right Hon. Lord Lawrence, Chairman

" ' of the Elementary Education Board.' "

" ' School Board for London,
" ' 33, New Bridge Street,
" ' June 22, 1871.
" ' Sir,
" ' I have the honour to acknowledge the receipt of your letter of the   June, and to inform you that it was laid before the Board yesterday, and referred by them to the Industrial Schools Committee. I will take care to inform you of their Report and the decision of the Board as soon as possible.
" ' I am, Sir,
" ' Your obedient Servant,
" ' J. W. Croad,
" ' Clerk of the Board.
" ' To Edmund E. Antrobus, Esq., J.P.,
" ' Sessions House,
" ' Clerkenwell.' "

" ' School Board for London,
" ' 33, New Bridge Steeet,
" ' August 4, 1871.
" ' Sir,
" ' I am directed by the School Board for London to say that they have carefully considered the question raised by your letter of the   June, and to reply that they have no present intention of establishing an Industrial School for girls.
" ' I am, Sir,
" ' Your obedient Servant,
" ' J. W. Croad,
" ' Clerk to the Board.
" ' To Edmund E. Antrobus, Esq., J.P.,
" ' Sessions House.' "

This latter letter from the Elementary School Board provides the Court with the information the Committee were instructed to obtain with respect to the intentions of that Board and the formation of Industrial Schools for girls.

Return of the number of girls under 16 years age committed to the Westminster Prison during the six years ending March, 1871.

The annexed return from the House of Correction, Westminster, will to some extent indicate the number of inmates it may be desirable to provide accommodation for. There are, however, numerous cases which come under the notice of both the Police and County Magistrates which would be sent to a county Industrial School if such an institution existed, and who are discharged, and who, consequently, at a later period become confirmed criminals.

Experience has demonstrated that it is not advisable or prudent to collect girls in large numbers in any institution, both with respect to their moral, religious education or industrial training, nor for a provision, when the time arrives for their obtaining employment, for their support. The erection of two or three buildings of a domestic character, to contain thirty, or at most fifty, inmates, would be ample for any district; and should it be 'expedient hereafter to provide for a larger number, it would be most desirable that accommodation should be found in another locality.

HOUSE OF CORRECTION, WESTMINSTER.

A Return showing the number and ages of girls under 16 years of age committed to the prison during the six years ending respectively at Michaelmas, 1866, 7, 8, 9, 70, and 71.

	1866	1867	1868	1869	1870	1871
Under 12 years of age ..	8	9	8	9	15	3
12 and under 14	34	20	26	28	29	1
14 and under 16	103	84	81	139	116	84
	145	113	115	176	160	103

Appointment of a Special Committee to provide an Industrial School under provisions of the Middlesex Act.

The appointment of a Special Committee in 1867, to consider the want of accommodation for girls in Reformatory and Industrial Schools; the offer of the Court to contribute a sum of £6,000 towards the establishment of a Reformatory School; and, lastly, the appointment of a Special Committee to provide an Industrial School, under the provisions of the Middlesex Act, in January last, proves that the Magistrates of the county of Middlesex retain the same interest in the reformation of juvenile offenders as their colleagues in 1853; and that they pursue the same enlightened policy which dictated their application to Parliament in 1854, and the principles embodied in the Act consequently obtained.

The reports of the Committees which have been presented to the Court, and which have been from time to time printed and circulated, furnish conclusive evidence of the urgent necessity for an institution to be established under one or more of the three statutes; and confirmation is obtained by a perusal of the returns of committals of the House of Correction, Westminster, and an extract from the fourteenth Report of the Inspector of Reformatory and Industrial Schools of Great Britain recently printed.

Extract from the fourteenth Report of the Inspector of Reformatory and Industrial Schools.

"It is much to be regretted that the proposed School for girls at Twickenham could not be carried out, the want of an additional Reformatory for this class of young offenders being very urgent, especially in the metropolitan districts. Every month now sees several girls left without means or opportunity of rescue from their vicious and criminal associates in London and its neighbourhood, there being no school into which they can be received; the criminal statistics of the year also showing an increase in the number of girls under 16 committed to prison, give reason for expecting that the demand for Reformatory accommodation for such offenders will become more urgent. I see at present, however, no prospect of any effort being made to supply the deficiency."

Absence of a Reformatory School in Middlesex for Girls of the Church of England.

It is a circumstance deeply to be regretted that in the Metropolitan county there is not a Reformatory School to which girls, who are members of the Church of England can be legally sent, the girls who are now sent to the Hampstead School, with which the Magistrates some few years since

made a contract under a misapprehension of its religious persuasion (being a Presbyterian School), are
so sent in violation of the 14th section of the 29th
and 30th Vict., cap. 117; the clause to which reference
is made runs thus :—

"In choosing a certified Reformatory School, the
Court, Justices, Magistrates, or Visiting Justices shall
endeavour to ascertain the religious persuasion to
which the youthful offender belongs, and, so far as
possible, a selection shall be made of a school conducted
in accordance with the religious persuasion to which
the youthful offender appears to the Court, Justice,
Magistrate, or Visiting Justice to belong, which persuasion shall be specified by the Court, Justice,
Magistrate, or Visiting Justice."

That the Roman Catholic children might be placed
in Roman Catholic Schools the Court of Quarter
Sessions has liberally contracted with the schools of
Mount St. Bernard and others, but with respect to
children of the Church of England only with two
schools, of a very limited character, capable of receiving not more than a dozen children, and those in
distant parts of the country. In order to ascertain the
amount of accommodation in the country for girls, the
Visiting Justices of the House of Correction caused a
letter to be written to the principal schools in other
counties; the replies, however, stated that very few
vacancies existed, and that the Managers declined to
make any permanent arrangement for even a limited
number of cases.

The present and the future for the consideration of the Magistrates. The question which now presents itself for the consideration of the Magistrates is the most effectual way to meet the urgent necessity for schools of a Reformatory and Industrial character. That it is urgent is fully stated in the reports of the several Committees appointed by the Court, the statistical information which has been obtained, and the Report of 1871 of the Inspector of Reformatories and Industrial Schools.

This subject has also fallen under the observation of the public press, and a very able article appeared in the 'Daily Telegraph' of the 28th of April last, of which the following is an extract.

Extract from the "Daily Telegraph" newspaper. "Is it not, then, surprising, when so much has been done for the boys, so little has been attempted for the girls? The rich and populous county of Middlesex has provided for the boys a really magnificent institution at Feltham. It works well in every sense, save, perhaps, that the parents of children who have been committed to Feltham by order of the Magistrates should not be allowed to regain possession of them when their time has expired. The poor boys often shrink from the claim with horror, but the parents are importunate and will not be denied. Such a result is a great evil, and surely the state and the county, which has fed, clothed, and trained the outcast for so many years, does actually stand in the place of the parent and should have a control over their future. Beyond this, so far as we know, Feltham works well, and has been of more advantage to the public than the addition of two or three thousand men to the Metropolitan Police Force. We have constantly heard rumours to the effect that the Middlesex Magistrates had taken, or were about to take, the case of the girls in hand; but as yet, nothing has been done. With the exception of four or five minute institutions—really the creation of private benevolence, though the directors may obtain the Government allowance for the children—there are no Industrial Schools for girls in the neighbourhood of London. We know of only one Reformatory as contra-distinguished from the Industrial School, it is at Hampstead; but though admirably managed, it is very limited in point of accommodation, and by no means helps us out of our difficulty. The subject should be looked to at once; it is second to no other in importance. What reasonable hope have we of diminishing the number of prostitutes in the London streets? We have dealt with the boy thieves *in esse* and *in posse*, and well have we been repaid for the outlay. Why should we not handle the difficult subject of prostitution in a similar manner, by sending the little waifs and strays of our gutters to school? It will be observed that we have carefully refrained from insisting on the moral and religious grounds which might have induced us to take speedy action. We take no higher ground than that of wise police regulations. Industrial Schools for the poor girls of London would be a first-rate investment, as our Industrial School for boys has already been. Why not get hold at once of the future mothers of thieves? The schoolmaster and mistress are better than a vigilant police."

Classification of girls for whom Reformatory and Industrial Schools are required.

The girls for whom Reformatory and Industrial schools are required may be advisedly placed in two classes: the first under fourteen years of age, and the second between fourteen and sixteen.

To meet the first cases the Court of Quarter Sessions has appointed a Special Committee to provide a school under the Middlesex Act, 17 and 18 Vict., cap. 169; and very great advantages are secured under the provisions of this Act.

The advantages of the Middlesex Act over the General, 29 & 30 Vict., c. 117.

Firstly.—The Court has full powers to purchase land or buildings, to erect schools, or to lease existing houses or schools.

Secondly.—To maintain the school and the inmates.

Thirdly.—The Institution, like the Lunatic Asylums and the Prisons, remains the property of the county.

Fourthly.—The management of a school under this Act is under the management of a Committee of Visitors (Magistrates) appointed by the Court.

Fifthly.—The inmates are sent direct from the Court of Quarter Sessions, Police Courts, or Petty Sessions without the degradation of imprisonment.

Lastly.—The Committee have the power to expend a sum not exceeding five pounds upon the boy or girl upon the termination of the period of detention in the school.

Considerable misapprehension appears to exist as to the powers of the Court over the age at which children may be sent to a school provided under the Act; although the Act limits it to children between the ages of seven and fourteen years, the Court is not precluded from confining the school to the reception of children at not less than twelve or thirteen, should such limitation appear essential for the welfare of the institution and the class of inmates for which it has been provided ; in the case of girls it would be advisable that only cases coming within the ages of twelve and fourteen years should be received, as the time of detention under the Act does not exceed three years, but which would under ordinary circumstances be sufficient ; the number of girls under twelve years of age coming under the notice of magistrates is extremely limited, and consequently no practical objection can arise.

Far greater difficulties present themselves in any effort which may be made to establish schools under either of the general Acts, 29 and 30 Vict., caps. 117 and 118, but as girls can be provided for under the Middlesex Act if under fourteen, it is only necessary to comment upon the provisions of the Reformatory Schools Act, cap. 117 :—

Firstly.—There must be an existing certified School or *bona fide* undertaking to provide one, before the Court of Quarter Sessions can make a contribution.

Secondly.— Contributions made to any certified School under the Act are handed over to a Committee of Managers, and become the property of the Managers, or their successors in the school.

Thirdly.—The Court can have no power over the management of the school, further than the withdrawing the amount of any weekly contribution which may be paid for the support of the inmates.

Fourthly.—The girls sent to a school under the

General Act, cap. 117, must be first subjected in every instance to the degradation of a committal for a period of not less than fourteen days to a prison; a provision utterly unworthy of an enlightened age.

At the present time there is not any Reformatory School in the county of Middlesex for the reception of girls, members of the Church of England, that at Hampstead being a Presbyterian School.

One of the lady visitors of one of our Metropolitan prisons thus writes:—

An appeal from a Lady Visitor of a prison. " There are surely few sadder things in this great London of ours than a visit to a women's prison. The sight of old hardened habituées, of middle-aged and young women, who will probably return in time no better; but saddest of all and most heart-breaking, that of very young girls (and little children occasionally) who are blasted, branded for life through the disgrace of being sent to such a place. That a child of eight, ten, or twelve years of age should be committed there at all is almost incredible, but the thing exists in this England of ours, and in the nineteenth century. What is to become of these children, friendless girls, and what is to be the future of these little ones who have seldom seen or heard aught but evil from their birth? Will they not go straight to destruction unless some help is given them? The Middlesex Magistrates have done much for boys—they have nobly given them every chance to right themselves and form good characters; the county cannot but rejoice over the hundreds who have been saved, through the Feltham Schools, from the degradation of a prison, and are now doing well; but the work is only half done while our girls are neglected, for if Industrial and Reformatory Schools are needed for boys, ten times more are they necessary for girls. It is possible for a boy to shift for himself and make his way in life even after having been in prison, but for girls it is far otherwise—without principle, without discipline, without a notion of truth, these wild girls require just double the amount of care, and better industrial training than our schools are accustomed to give--sound religious teaching, and a happier faith than is to be found out of the pale of the Church of England. Fearful is the amount of influence a bad woman has in the world, incalculable the mischief she can do; on the other hand, if good, her influence is felt and tends to the temporal and eternal welfare of all classes who may surround her. Give the girls an equal chance with the boys, and the recompense will be the same. It is a rare thing to find one really hardened or without some good, and the result of many years' experience convinces me that a large percentage of the young who may commit offences may, with care, be rescued from a life of misery and become useful and respected members of society."

Extract from the Report of the Special Committee of the House of Commons on the Prison Ministers Acts. In illustration, the following paper, printed in the report of the Select Committee of the House of Commons on Prisons and Prison Ministers Acts, will not be without interest. It is the result of my work of nine years :—

" During nine years, from 1861 to the end of 1869,

230 prisoners have been visited in their cells; of these 8 are married, 26 are known to be satisfactory, 39 were last heard of in refuges or schools, and were also doing well, 103 have not been heard of at all since leaving prison; but as a great part of these returned at once to friends or home, there is reason to hope they have not returned to crime; 15 are still in homes, 12 are unsatisfactory, 22 have returned to prison, but only 2 for more than once, and 3 of those are now married and going on well, and 14 are still in prison, and 1 in Hanwell.

"I believe the falling into crime in most instances to have arisen from the want of proper homes, good parents, and education. Many girls of 17 and 18 could neither read nor write; two had never heard of Jesus Christ before going to prison; 60 had one parent only; 43 were orphans or friendless; 44 were foreigners—chiefly Germans from Whitechapel or the City Road; 35 were almost totally ignorant; 151 were under 20 years of age, and 6 under 12. Of those who returned to prison, 10 gave little hope from the first, two being amongst the most refractory prisoners; 9 refused to go to a refuge or home, and returned immediately to bad companions from prison."

In order, however, to give effect to the instructions by the Court of Quarter Sessions to the Special Committee, that efforts should be made to establish a school under the General Act, and for this purpose to invite subscriptions as before stated, a second independent Committee has been formed, to establish a school for girls, under which one or other of the General Acts, notwithstanding the difficulties and

imperfections attached to them, and in reply to an
appeal to their brother Magistrates, a sum of nearly
£800 has been already subscribed.   Liberal as the
response has been, it is inadequate to establish a
school, except upon a most limited scale, even if a
contribution is added under the Act by the Court.

*Practical sug-
gestion for the
consideration of
the Magistrates
for the estab-
lishment of
Industrial
Reformatory
Schools for Girls
in the county of
Middlesex.*   The important question for the Court
of Quarter Sessions to consider is, that
having provided a school for boys which
has proved eminently successful, shall the
girls be neglected altogether, as at present ?   The following appears a practical
solution of the question : that the Special
Committee be instructed to provide an institution of a domestic character, under the Middlesex
Act, for a number not exceeding one hundred, or at
most, one hundred and fifty; this would provide for
girls under the age of 14.   The independent Committee would then be in a position to devote the funds
at their present disposal and contributions that will
hereafter be received to supplement the Institution,
with a school to receive those above that age.

In conclusion, and in reply to observations which
have been made with respect to the site recommended
by the Special Committee in their Report of April
last, the following remarks are sufficient to confirm the
selection made by the Committee :—

First. The site is within a few hundred yards of a
    first-class railway station, but so removed from
    it, that no possible inconvenience would arise,
    while all its advantages would be available.

Second. The soil is gravel, the situation most
healthy, and the supply of water excellent, and
in any quantity, to be had from wells, and from
the stream which supplies Hampton Court Palace with water, which is the boundary of one
side of the plot.

Third. The sewage can be utilised as at the School
at Feltham, the soil being the same and pecu-
liarly adapted for its reception.

Fourth. The price of the land, considering its
situation, is moderate.

Fifth. In reply to the objection to the site, that it
is in dangerous proximity to the school at Feltham, and that the name of the place would be
prejudicial, it must be stated that the site is
nearly two miles distant from it, and that two
schools are already in the immediate neighbourhood of the County School for both boys and
girls, and further, that schools of a charitable
and philanthrophic character are known more by
name than by their locality.

Sixth. That facilities given for the meeting of
Committees by being close to a first-class railway
station is most important, not only to the Members of the Committee, but to the due management of an institution.

It is in the power of the Court to purchase any
quantity of land not exceeding one hundred acres for
a school. The plot of land recommended by the
Committee consists of only seventeen acres, and is
surrounded by an excellent fence; and although,
strictly speaking, a smaller quantity would suffice,
still it would be very desirable that the whole should

be purchased, firstly, for the utilisation of the sewage; and secondly, to secure privacy. The value of land increasing, should the seventeen acres not be required at a future time, any surplus might be sold at an increased price.

The amount already subscribed by the Magistrates and their friends, as shown in the annexed list, already amounts to nearly eight hundred pounds, which would be doubtless increased to fifteen hundred if the Court would contribute a site at a nominal rent for a term of years part of land which might be purchased for a school under the Middlesex Act. This sum of fifteen hundred pounds would be sufficient to erect a small domestic building for the reception of thirty girls, and for which a certificate, under the 29 and 30 Vict., cap. 117, would be granted by the Government. By an arrangement of this nature the building would ultimately become the property of the county; and the Court (the school being established) would have the power, not only to contribute towards the support of the inmates, but to assist in the extension, if required, at a future time.

Finally. The Magistrates who have read these pages will find that the necessity of an institution for the reception of girls is reported by no less than three Special Committees appointed by the Court, by the returns from our prisons, and by the last report of the Inspector of Reformatory and Industrial Schools. The Court has shown an earnest desire to provide a refuge for the neglected girls—first, on the recommendation of a Special Committee, acting under a misapprehension of the provisions of the General Act, 29 and 30 Vict., cap. 117, in offering to contribute the sum of six thousand pounds towards an illegal and impracticable scheme—which scheme, however, collapsed, and the Magistrates were saved the humiliating defeat, which would inevitably have followed the application for a mandamus in the Court of Queen's Bench; and, secondly, in the appointment of a Special Committee to provide an Industrial School, under the provisions of the Middlesex Act: and thus sustaining those benevolent and enlightened views which have for so many years distinguished the Magistrates of the metropolitan county.

The course suggested in these pages comes strictly within the provisions of both the Middlesex Act and those of the General Act, 29 and 30 Vict., cap. 117, and carries out the recommendation of the Court, that efforts should be made to establish a school under the provisions of the latter Act, which the members of the independent Committee have zealously forwarded, as will be seen by the list of contributions; will provide schools for both classes, and enable the Magistrates to carry out the benevolent object they have in view, and supply that want which is now so urgently required, and, without intruding on the very limited space which is occasionally at the disposal of managers of institutions which the liberality of the benevolent have established in other and distant counties.

INDEPENDENT COMMITTEE.

The Committee of Promoters consists of the following Magistrates :—

EDMUND EDWARD ANTROBUS, Esq., Chairman, J.P.

THE MOST NOBLE THE MARQUIS OF WESTMINSTER.

HENRY POWNALL, Esq., J.P., late Chairman of the Quarter Sessions.

SIR WILLIAM HENRY BODKIN, Assistant Judge, J.P.

JOHN GILLIAM STILWELL, Esq., J.P.

JOHN GILBERT TALBOT, Esq., M.P., J.P.

THOMAS LUCAS, Esq., J.P.

GEORGE MOORE, Esq., J.P.

JOHN F. FRANCE, Esq., J.P.

HENRY JOHN BAXTER, Esq., J.P.

BENJAMIN JOHN ARMSTRONG, Esq., J.P.

JAMES HOLBERT WILSON, Esq., J.P.

HENRY GRIFFITH, Esq., J.P.

HENRY EDWARD PELLEW, Esq., J.P.

ROBERT DIMSDALE, Esq., M.P., J.P.

SIR JAMES TYLER, J.P.

GENERAL TREMENHEERE, J.P.

H. H. SEYMOUR, Esq., J.P.

J. E. L. BRANDRETH, Esq., J.P.

Subscriptions will be received by Edmund E. Antrobus, Esq., 14, Kensington Palace Gardens, W.; or by the Honorary Secretary, Mr. Charles Wright, Sessions House, Clerkenwell, E.C.

LIST OF CONTRIBUTIONS

RECEIVED TO THE PRESENT TIME.

	£	s.
The Duke of Wellington, Apsley House, Piccadilly ..	50	0
The Marquis of Westminster, Grosvenor House ..	100	0
Edmund E. Antrobus, Esq., J.P., 14, Kensington Palace Gardens	20	0
J. G. Stilwell, Esq., J.P., 33, Gordon Square	20	0
Sir James Tyler, J.P., Pine House, Holloway.. ..	60	0
John Norbury, Esq., J.P., (late). 30, Gorden Square ..	10	0
Lord Ebury, J.P., 107, Park Street, Grosvenor Square	10	0
Charles Hill, Esq., J.P., 29, Threadneedle Street ..	5	0
Thomas Lucas, Esq., J.P., 13, Kensington Palace Gardens	20	0
W. H. Smith, Esq., M.P., J.P., 1, Hyde Park Street..	20	0
J. G. F.	5	0
J. Noble, Esq., J.P., 50. Westbourne Terrace.. ..	20	0
Thomas G. Sambrooke, Esq., J.P. (late), 32, Eaton Place	5	0
George Norbury, Esq., 30. Gordon Square	5	0
H. John Baxter, Esq., J.P., 5, Pembridge Villas, Bayswater	5	0
Henry Pellew, Esq., J.P., 22, Boltons, West Brompton	10	0
Miss Antrobus, 14, Kensington Palace Gardens ..	5	0
Henry Pownall, Esq.. J.P.. 63, Russell Square ..	10	0
George Moore, Esq., J.P., 15, Kensington Palace Gardens	20	0
John F. France, Esq., J.P., 2, Norfolk Terrace ..	5	5
The Assistant Judge, J.P.. West Hill, Highgate ..	10	0
Henry Griffith, Esq., J.P., 30, Princes Gardens, Hyde Park	10	0
J. A. Shaw Stewart, Esq., J.P., 13, Queen's Gate ..	10	0
Sir Walter Farquhar, Baronet, J.P., King Street, St. James's	5	0
Stephen Kennard, Esq., J.P., Woodlands, Harrow Weald, Stanmore	10	10
James H. Wilson, Esq., J.P., 19, Onslow Square ..	10	0
Raikes Currie, Esq., J.P., 67, Lombard Street.. ..	20	0
Augustin Robinson, Esq., J.P., West Lavant House Chichester	10	0
Total	£490	15

	£	s.
Brought forward	490	15
Richard Twining, Esq., J.P., J.P., 215, Strand	10	0
Jos. Pugh, Esq., J.P., 23, Lancaster Gate, Hyde Park	10	0
Miss Wcod, New Lodge, Reigate	5	0
Richard Nicholson, Esq., Clerk of the Peace, Sessions House, Clerkenwell	5	0
Baron Lionel M. de Rothschild, M.P., J.P., 148, Piccadilly	20	0
Miss E. M. Antrobus, 14, Kensington Palace Gardens	5	0
Mrs. Willis, 33, Gordon Square..	5	0
J. Gurney Hoare, Esq., J.P., Child's Hill, Hampstead	10	0
Angus Croll, Esq., J.P., Granard Lodge, Roehampton	10	0
William Murray, Esq., J.P., 11, Cambridge Square ..	10	0
William Bird, Esq., J.P.	5	0
John J. J. Stilwell, Esq., Arundel Street, Strand ..	5	0
Henry Stilwell, Esq., Arundel Street, Strand	5	0
Lady Bodkin, West Hill, Highgate	5	0
Charles White, Esq., J.P., Barnesfield, Stone	5	0
Charles S. Butler, Esq., J.P. (late), Cazenoves, Upper Clapton..	10	0
G. F. Franco, Esq., J.P. (late), Eaton Place	5	0
Sir F. Lycett, J.P., 18, Highbury Grove	5	0
Robert Holland, Esq., J.P., Stanmore Hall, Great Stanmore	20	0
Edward Warner, Esq., J.P., 49, Grosvenor Place ..	5	0
Hugh H. Seymour, Esq., J.P., 30, Upper Brook Street	5	5
Edward W. Cox, Esq., J.P., Deputy Assistant Judge, Moat House, Highwood, Hendon	5	0
Sir William Tite, J.P., 42, Lowndes Square	10	0
J. Kelk, Esq., J.P., 109, Lancaster Gate	10	0
J. F. Pownall, Esq., J.P., 63, Russell Square	5	0
E. W. Wadeson, Esq., J.P., 40, Tavistock Square ..	5	0
E. L. Brandreth, Esq., J.P., 32, Elvaston Place, Queen's Gate, Kensington	5	0
P. P. Blyth, Esq., J.P., 53, Wimpole Street	5	0
G. Ashley Dodd, Esq., J.P., 40, St. James's Street ..	20	0
Thomas Scott, Esq., J.P., Nevill Park, Tunbridge Wells	10	0
Sir John Kirkland, J.P. (late), Eaton Place	5	0
Mrs. Brown, Lancaster Gate	2	2
G. C.	5	0
Total	£743	2

www.ingramcontent.com/pod-product-compliance
Lightning Source LLC
Chambersburg PA
CBHW022040080426
42733CB00007B/910